FEAR COUNTRY

FEAR COUNTRY

A journey from lost to mostly found

Poems by

ALICE EWENS

Cover designed by Alice Ewens utilising royalty free stock photography and fonts available through Adobe Spark.
Cover photo – @aaronburden via Unsplash
Cover font – Cabin Sketch
Internal font - Garamond

First Printing, 2019
ISBN 9781790931118
For more, see www.alicewroteit.com /
@alicewroteit for Facebook and Instagram

For Dad
Sorry it's late

For James
Thank you for being my compass

"The clearest way into the Universe
is through a forest wilderness."
- John Muir

Contents

3: Homeward

1: Lost

*"I came to myself,
in a dark wood,
where the direct way was lost"*
Dante Alighieri (The Divine Comedy)

Jam Jar Heart

"How can you stand the vastness of this wind-whipped sky?"
I asked, terrified.
"Open", she replied, "Just open."
I'm afraid to try.

Forecast

This old winter regret makes my bones ache.
Ugly shadows are on the way.
Depression is a winter-smothered silence,
Anxiety is its cruel biting wind.
I am hollow and old.
There is no warmth in these cold hallways
Of echoes and memories.
I carry it in my pocket all the time,
In my rib cage,
In my spine.
Sometimes it leaks from my eyes.
I'm catching tears on Sundays,
Like I could've caught them all along if I'd just tried harder.
I've been trying hard my whole life and I'm often out of breath
From all the compartments of my flooded heart struggling to stay afloat.
My heart has often sat low in the waves,
But I can't write this many poems about the ocean
And not know a thing or two about the tide -
It finds a way to bring the water back to me.
Everything comes back, eventually.

Creeping Dose

We met in a nightclub,
Nothing special, nothing new, except you would not stop smiling
Like the very threads of fate were tugging at the corners of your face.
Me, in my cracked leather and held-together-with spit-and-a-prayer,
You kept staring at my hair,
Like this was it, our forever walking out the door - -
And I could no more dig my heels in and refuse
Than gravity can refuse the floor.
Every night curled in against the love song of your skin,
Carve our names into a tree,
Like the Universe…lured us into a false sense of security,
Like the Universe saw us wrapped inside our sappy, happy-ever-
Never-gonna-let-you-go,
And the Universe said *Hell No.*
A year of everything is pure and good, and then
Words dropping from your mouth like rotting wood.
Surgery, six months of chemo and then *maybe* you might be well.
I wonder if you could tell
That I was crying when I told you we'd get through this,
Like this is how the world ends,
Not with a bang but a ten-minute phone call and a diagnosis.
This. Is how. The world ends.
Like suddenly knowing I don't know anything anymore.
My spine's ripped out and I'm gutted, boneless on the floor,
Like my heart is homeless and how do I ever start
To pick up the pieces of our forever and put them in a jar?
And then it's endless waiting and navigating hospital corridors,
Like all the patients with their internal wars
Swallow bile and choke and hope that this week won't be so bad,
And the shop assistant thinks I'm mad, when I shout
At the most ridiculous woolly hat I'm picking for when your hair falls out.
I find you staring into this hazy middle ground,

[…]

Like you're so lost that you don't want to be found,
Like staring at the surface of the sun,
Like the echoing sound of a fired gun hits me in the gut
When you don't even want me to touch you, *but - -*
I make you chalk stars and origami cranes and finally,
You smile at me when I make you paper planes,
And there is so much beauty in the world,
So much beauty curled around the darkest fangs of fear,
Like we can hear the church bells on Sunday,
And we make love all day on Monday just to feel alive,
But I'm holding my breath, treading water, trying not to sink,
Like, you can only drink water now 'cause you told me how
Your hands hurt too much to hold a mug of tea,
And I might be running around keeping track
Of every appointment and pack of drugs,
But the fear tugs incessantly.
I'm waiting to know if this is it,
Like knowing but not saying it that Christmas will be shit,
But what if we never get another one together?
So I put fairy lights around your door
And tell you there will never be anything more
Perfect to me than Hark the Herald Angels Sing and strawberry pudding,
'Cause that's all you can eat without being sick,
And I'm so fucking tired of waiting and skating on thin ice,
Like feeling the very marrow of my bones is stretched on a piano wire,
And the chords stretch higher until I want to gouge out my eyes,
'Cause I'm tired of the lies I put in them,
Like I'm OK and I'm coping and I'm strong...
But that's wrong.
I'm not coping,
I'm just hoping to make it through 'til it's time to leave,
Without wanting to scream blue rage into the night,
Like there's no way *this* can be right.
You're twenty-seven and nothing
Rhymes with cancer.

Way Down We Go

Lonely doesn't have to be alone.
Everything changes.
There are few things as crushing as the silence.
Saturday morning when you wake up,
And wonder about the happy moments.
That strange incurable ache,
Can be a terrible weight.
Simply the
Everyday business of
You and me.

Fever Moon

There are still nights
When my body refuses your sacred touch.
There is too much demon in my blood.
You ask me why I can never
Love you with the lights on.
I tell you I am scared you'll see
The dotted guidelines that let him
Turn me into cuts of meat
From ribs and thigh and belly,
When, spread upon a butcher's block,
He took my chubby girlish barely-bloomed humility
And dropped it in some midnight parking lot
With ruined cold asphalt grazes on my knees.
The ghosts of these festered wounds winding
Twenty-years of shame
That I am still trying to douse in gasoline.
On these hot nights, my skin burns with it.
The earth is split and spits dust
To the fever moon.
The taste of it lingers in the
Wasteland of discarded bodies.
You hold me holy.
You hold me whole.
My chest swells with the weight of it.
I leave windows open so I can breathe.

Precipice

And when the precipice opens
Beneath your feet
(Because it will),
Remember to howl like the wild thing you are
Into the heart of your dying star.
Call all your dark matter and raging fire home.
Close wounds with spider silk ripped from your own hunter's bow.
Breath deep
And carry on.
The ravine is not that deep,
I promise.
It's just
Another precipice.

The Marvellous Mechanical Wind Up Man

Hi Dad,
I got you a card.
It was hard.
I mean, it's been a while since we spoke.
It's been a while since your crooked tooth jokes,
Since your crooked mouth laugh was a prize,
Since I saw your sea-storm eyes crinkle,
Since you called me "kid",
Since you suddenly skidded sidelong from "a bit tired" into
Cancer-dying-gone.
Eleven weeks from diagnosis,
Eleven weeks of what's this, hang on, *wait*, what the *hell* is going on?
Followed by radio silence and six months of static.
Six months of my life in automatic.
Six months of trying to find these scattered ship-wrecked pieces
And wait for them to fit into something new.
How do I find a way to fit into an existence without you?
I can't find the words to explain the way
My brain fills with the pain of sitting beside you,
Holding your hand and watching you transform like shifting sand
Into the "Marvellous Mechanical Wind-up Man",
Hearing the cogs and wheels in your tin-man chest refuse to rest,
And, sure if you could move, I'd find a huge brass key in your back too,
Slowly tic-tock-click-clacking and winding down,
Breaths pulled in and pumped out and in and out and in and...out,
Until I wanted to scream just to make some other sound than you
Clattering and rattling downhill and...
There's something wrong.
Major Tom, your clockwork stopped.
And the stars gently weep on Christmas Eve,
When there's this jagged-edged hole where my dad used to be.
So we drink too much tea,

[...]

Fill stockings with ash and tears and broken hearts,
Wrap shattered parts in years of nicotine-stained memories
And T-shirts gone soft after too many times in the wash.
I found a whole cupboard filled with every tie I ever bought you -
Every book and CD and letter and story and poem I ever sent you,
Every word you read like it could free you,
Every awkward teenage lie I told you,
Every Father's Day card I ever gave you,
Every tiny little girl fist reaching out for a hand to hold, you
Never threw anything out!
Cluttered up my life with peanut butter on toast and rock and blues and
That time you were in a rush and went out in odd shoes,
And the music, *and the music*, and *all* the music
Was a soundtrack to our lives,
Long car drives and stupid jokes that no one ever got,
And all the half-empty paint pots
Stashed in a cupboard with every single fucking tie
You ever owned, I swear!
I remembered every story you ever told me,
Including the one about the time you did 'shrooms
And giggled for twelve hours,
Pressed those memories between the pages of my history
Like soft flowers.
Dad I could've cried for hours,
But I tied about ten of those ties around my head
And rocked out with you to Floyd instead.
Dad, you taught me to always rock out instead.
Dad I'm sorry I got blisters on my lips
from all the things we never said.
Dad I miss you,
And I think it's going to be a long time
Until I'm anywhere near fine,
My feet going over old ground and old fears,
And I'm doing my best, but I wish you were here,
I wish you'd never left.

Roommates

Depression lumps itself around me, overstuffed and bloated,
Coating every inch in waxy, oily, clinging, molasses.
Depression is the thumb-print bruises beneath my eyes.
Depression steals all the covers in the night,
Throws heavy limbs across my chest and makes sure I know
My body is a glass paperweight at best -
A dome of frozen air and molten sharp things.
My depression is cotton-wool mouth mumbling
As I stumble through a copy of a copy of a copy of each day.
Depression is an empty corridor of nothing.
It's not a war, it's a field-hospital trauma room full of dead things,
And when Depression is sure my feet have turned into lead,
Anxiety takes up residence as an extra uninvited guest.
Anxiety is the irrational frantic yapping terrier to
Depression's lumbering great dane of a black dog.
Anxiety hangs off me in billowing trailing waves.
Anxiety races through the house screaming
In a never-ending wailing siren of panic.
Anxiety and Depression both agree I'm not much of a hostess,
Tell me I'm worthless,
Tell me to remember every bad choice I've ever made since I was six,
Tell me I can't be trusted with nice things
Like self-esteem, like love, like hope…
Tell me it's all my fault and the truth of that is a rope.
When Grief finally shows up to the party years later,
The other two bow down in servility,
Then rise up like bile, like smoke and ghosts,
But Grief doesn't bully, doesn't chide,
Grief helps me sink to my knees and says *"I know. You're right."*
And that is so much worse.
Grief is a tremble, a deep ocean hurt, a pickaxe.
Grief is an ice-cream scoop gouging out the back of my throat.
Grief is a trapped howl, a silence, a gap.

Heart Shaped Box

You think me some dark muse,
Choose to see me wrapped in smoke and feathers,
Your elemental witch.
I am not your silver-spun heart trinket,
Stop looking for me by candlelight.
There is nothing romantic in tragedy.
I am nothing more than a bloodied rag
Pressed to the gash in your side.
I unwind myself from a desperate sleep
And try to keep the creaking from my brittle bones as,
Homeless, I twist into the next shape needed of me.
If only I could tame these wolves
Howling at the cave of my chest.
The wild hurricane of midnight wings
Calls me from myself.
The whispers of a forgotten place,
A misplaced memory
Locked in some half-searched world,
Some rush of truth glancing blows off forgotten sleep.
Once, in a dream, I greeted
The wilderness as a friend.
Once, somewhere deep and long grown dim,
I knew the wilderness within.

The Exact Shade of Red

My mother once gave me
A little ceramic plaque that said
"Be as brilliant as your Mum thinks you are".
I should point out I'd have to go pretty far
For my Mum to not think I'm some kind of wonder-kid.
My Mum thinks I could literally roll a shit in glitter
And it would deserve to sit on a pedestal in the Louvre.
I mean, that's what Mum's do, right? but still,
Mum, it's a tough act to fill.
Trip-dancing between a scared little girl and
The woman seeping out through the cracks,
Still wanting to climb into your lap,
Still drawing your strength up through my roots like sap,
Flawed and fragile and still so far from ready to be all that,
And still so very aware that maybe,
Now you need me
To be that brilliant supernova that you think I am.
I hold your hands
And count the years in your concentric rings.
I hold your hobbled soft body to me
As we slow dance in your kitchen
And I say "I love you" and what I mean is
"Don't ever leave".
What I mean is
"My heart will never be ready to grieve
The enormity of you going".
You were always supermassive black hole to me,
The centre of my Universe, the centre of my gravity,
Always the teeth-and-tits grin,
Lipstick-and-no-bullshit puckered on your mug of tea.
Mamma, now you're tiny,
Dwarf star,

[...]

Finds me resting my chin on your talcum-powder hair,
Finds me watching you leant against the sink doing dishes,
Thinking you've grown up into your own mother -
The way you laugh like her,
The way you heave your tired legs over my threshold like her,
Always climbing right in to where I'm at
Just to kiss it better,
Always setting my world to rights,
Setting tears to a soundtrack of old songs on the radio -
Sweet Home Alabama and Red Red Wine,
Until we're fine for a time.
I'm afraid my heart is too full of needing you
To ever learn to let go of your elegant oak-tree hand,
To ever learn to stand on my own two daisy-chain feet,
To ever stop having those dreams of
Running after you in the street,
Seeing your back disappear round corners and bookstacks
In the green woollen coat you've long since gifted me.
See, I'll always be waiting to grow into everything you've shed,
Trying to climb inside the exact shade of red
You wore like armour,
Trying to galvanise my core and withstand the event horizon,
Knowing I'm not sure I'll ever be
As brilliant as you deserve me to be.

Rusted

My rust-coiled hair slides through his fingers.
He lingers at my temples,
He knows I leave collection plates there for the fear,
Offerings to some vast thing,
Begging please, please, *please*...
My red-knuckled hands hold his and
He rests now.
The tests and tubes and all the rest
Done for now,
And all is well.
For now.
This oxidised well-worn worry
Put back in its box,
Vestments folded and stored,
The ritual complete once more.
For now.

Unmake This Wild Light

These days I'm an old shirt
Gone through the wash too many times,
Too stretched, too big and clumsy to fit into my smile.
Gone are the days when I was cast iron and black lace,
Striding out in blossomed ink all wild haloed hair,
When lightning filled my blood
And a Universe filled my throat,
When I filled pages with constellations
And they watched me like weathermen.
I cannot breathe here anymore.
I sip air like I might blow out this guttering candle,
Sputtering, tripping over truths and scars that
Drop from my mouth like tiny cold round river pebbles.
Now I am a marble curled in upon myself,
With eyes too big and hands too slow
To cover all the naked curves of my sharp skin.
I have become the copper penny taste of panic
Lurching up in the battlefield of my bed
For my nightly forty rounds with doubt.
I am ground to dust.
I am forgetting my own name.
Shame and all its ghosts trail me through every crowd.
These days I'm nothing more than glass and spider-silk.
Don't breathe too loud.

Anxiety 101

You left your umbrella at the bus stop, or possibly in Tesco, this morning,
The *really good* umbrella,
The big one that you sort of stole/"borrowed long term" from the back
of your husband's car,
And you don't know if you left it at the bus stop when you got off the bus
and awkwardly stopped to re-button your coat,
Because, at 31 years old, you still have mornings when you just can't do
buttons,
Or whether you left it in Tesco propped up by the self-service till,
After attempting to fit 3 days of breakfast and lunch into a tiny handbag,
Because, at 31 years old, sometimes you still can't forward-plan and pack
a tote bag,
Even though you packed a tote bag yesterday,
And now it's taking slightly too long to fit your stuff in your bag, Tetris-
style,
And the security guard is looking at you like he thinks maybe you're trying
to smuggle more packets of ramen noodles that you paid for
Into the ever-shrinking-handbag,
So you scurry off carrying a bag of porridge oats under one arm...
And then realise halfway down the street and halfway across the road
That you no longer have your umbrella,
And you're too crippled with self-loathing at your own ineptitude that you
can't bring yourself to run back into Tesco or to the bus stop,
So you don't,
And then you almost do,
Dithering on the crossing,
Until the lights change and you almost get run over,
Because Bristol drivers do not understand a low level panic attack
Halfway across Park Street at 8am on a Wednesday,
And this just throws off your entire game all day,
Because it was a *really* good umbrella.

Of Socks and Clocks

This world is too bright, too harsh, to raw for me.
It stings like a grazed knee.
Let me curl up in the safe warm tea-and-toast,
Make the most of warm socks and steady clocks
Tick-tocking reliably.
My barefoot soul is bruised,
Second-hand and used,
Dirt ground into all the swirls of my identity,
Waiting for a summer storm to wash it clean.
Tell me it is OK to wait and breathe and just…be.
It's not like I don't know the meaning of wilful naivety.

Ghosts In The Walls

Shame hammers me concave,
Rounds my shoulders,
Curved and hunched,
With aching, crooked vertebrae,
Until I am an empty bowl
Echoing and cold as a cathedral in winter.
You could hear a pin drop in the caverns
Of my inadequacy.
There are ghosts in my walls, see.
Listen.
I am hollow as a carved pumpkin,
All the glistening things that grow
Now scooped away.
Stay.
There are ghosts in my walls
Whispering white noise.
My panic is more retreat than attack,
And yet more bite than bark,
More shivering gooseflesh on bare arms
Holding themselves in the dark.
My grandmother would say someone
Walked over my grave.
The ghosts of all the women who came before
Refusing to be bowed,
Or cowed,
Or made small by their own short falls -
Their sepia stained regal stares
Dare me to walk tall.
These cast iron women,
Waists made wasp-like,
Buzzing bees beneath steel and satin and
Tightly-bound breath,

[…]

Like, beyond death, they might uncoil in some great explosion
Of unshed tears and hardships born,
White haired witch crone sisters in mourning-black,
Boot-button eyes made shiny bright and staring back,
Holding everything in focus,
Holding every truth up to the light to look for holes.
Their fight, their steel
Bristles in my veins.
There are ghosts in my walls.
Here.
Can you feel them?
Can you hear what they say?
Such salt in my blood,
Urging me to unfold my shoulders,
Unwrap my hunched frame.
The weight of their gaze
Is heavy
All the same.

The Woman Who

I have been many things and played many parts,
Juggled hearts and spare parts,
Been both the kite and the lightning strike.
I, the woman who chose you.
I, the woman who knew, somehow,
You were worth a hundred thunderstorms
If you'd only ask me to dance in the rain.
I, the woman who saw the first flickers of pain
Cloud your ocean eyes.
I, the woman who stayed when death came knocking
For you from the inside,
Tied you to your train track scars as the drugs dripped
Like we were Icarus trying our luck with the sun.
I, the woman with the loaded gun balanced precariously in my rib cage;
The smell of cordite when we kissed.
I, the woman who sat frayed, raw, aching.
I, the woman who dragged the sky down to fill you with air
When you said the fire in your veins was suffocating.
I, with the white surrender flag waving from my own parapet
When it dawned on me that a life is more than staying alive.
I, the woman who played brave and told you we'd get married
The day you found a way to crawl back to me.
I, the woman who waited,
Who dug my own trenches and
Bedded down for the duration of that war,
Never sure what we had won and lost along the way,
But grateful anyway to be hollow-eyed survivors.
I, the woman who grew knives for bones,
Learnt to carve fear into words and clear cool water,
Taught you to wash the pain away in me.
I, the woman who wore red on our wedding day.
I, who dared to love,

[...]

Knowing life can crack like eggshell,
Knowing hell is the waiting room,
Knowing every second is a gift,
Knowing this life, love, is your battered body
And my half-tattered heart
Just holding on,
Just holding the jagged parts together.

Wilderness Survival Guide

1. Watch Zombie movies. When eyeing exits and escape routes, as anxiety comes crawling up the inside of your throat, you can tell people you are figuring out how to zombie-proof the room. They'll probably think it's cute. It might even fill your mouth with words that stop the panic escaping.

2. You will talk too much when you are anxious. Your words will tumble like wet jewels of innards tumbling from split guts. Your words will sound claxon sirens.

3. Some days you will be a holy temple in a sea of tranquillity, a superhuman tour de force. Some days the sum of your achievements will be retrieving the TV remote from under the bed and eating peanut butter from the jar. Make sure there's always peanut butter.

4. In the event of a complete system failure, find a toilet stall and lock yourself in it. Count tiles. Focus on the grouting. Brace arms for impact.

5. Expect grief like a summer storm. Don't leave home without an umbrella.

6. Never, under any circumstances, leave home without earphones. They will be more important than the umbrella. Music can save you.

7. Pick up pieces of fallen sunshine as you go. Fill pockets with them. Fill whole rooms. There will be times when this glow will be the only thing to keep you going. Keep going.

8. Learn to make fire from every harsh word you ever told yourself. Rub those lies together until they spark a light. They will keep you warm through the darkest of nights.

[...]

9. When your centre does not look like it can hold its breath long enough to make it to the uncracked ground, there is an elegance to be found in the uncertainty. Embrace it.

10. On the occasions when you cannot hear yourself, when you have returned all the unread love notes and unheard mixtapes in a box left by your own front door, when the light of you is turned away, when the bright sun of you is eclipsed by darkness, when you crumble in the shadow and gasp for air on the dark side of your lightning loops, when the panicked moth of your soul beats itself bloody on sound-proof glass...ride out this storm. You won't hear yourself until it's time to. Wait for your light to come back around. The light will always come back around.

2: Map Reading and Route Finding

"The wound is where the light enters you."
Rumi

Falling Leaves

See how brave that leaf is?
Holds its breath and just...
Lets go.
I know that's easier said than done.
The dawn cannot let go of the sun.

Unexpected Roses

In the drawn-out drought of misery,
In the cracked dirt and dry yellowed grass of grief,
In the space left untended,
Across a lawn more moss and dandelions gone to seed,
I take a barefoot walk
To feel the deep hurt between my toes.
High time I got to know the feel of it again,
High time to once more tend
This sprawling spot of sunburnt daisies,
And there, despite the lack of care,
Despite the arid air and white-bone sky,
A burst of unexpected roses climbing high.
Perfect painted petals of
Apricots and cream.
A sudden burst of life in this too-stretched heat,
Like a long cool drink after the driest desert night.
I don't expect anything so joyful to grow here.
I don't expect soft petals bowing their heads,
Don't expect to laugh so delightedly
At these wanton hanging yellow globes.
I don't expect to know such peace in this wild place,
Yet here it is,
As quiet and unassuming as a
Weather-wizened face.
Even in the most desolate and lonely places,
I suppose eventually some sweet-smelling things will always grow.
The gentlest memories unfurl in soft corollas,
And grateful as I am
For unexpected roses
In this landscape of the lost.

This Is Fear Country

I'm going to let you in on a secret.
I'm afraid of everything.
I mean it.
Spiders (obviously); cockroaches; chickens;
The sounds my house makes in the night; heights;
Falling - I fall over a lot, but getting that much practice
Doesn't stop me being afraid of tripping,
So I hold on so tight I get blisters from my panic attacks.
I'm afraid of missed phone calls -
Only call me if you're *literally* dying or -
Yeah, I'm afraid of dying, or -
You may have noticed, I have a very fertile imagination.
It has teeth.
I mean, I'm afraid of crowds and loud sounds -
I spent every firework display as a kid
Swaying with my fingers rammed in my ears,
Desperately trying to hold my brain in when the sky exploded.
I'm afraid of tornadoes and tidal waves,
And small spaces and boats and flying and...*toddlers*...
And the freaks that get elected,
And leaving old teabags in the bottom of the jar
In case they feel neglected,
And aliens, and corporations and ghosts,
And of being boring.
At school I was afraid of scoring too highly on tests because, get this,
I was afraid of being "best".
Yes, it was a decided unlike for being in any kind of spotlight, but also
Lest I give myself a higher stage to fall from.
I have always been afraid of falling,
Which is to say I have always been afraid of failing.
I've never been good enough at sea to fill my own sails,

[...]

My legs never steady enough to withstand my own earthquakes.
See, I'm afraid I feel too much,
And when I try to stop,
I'm left clutching at paper dolls with straw for hair
Screaming "need me, *need me*",
I'm scared that no one needs me,
And I'm afraid that everyone has already said everything I have to say,
Only said it better.
If only I could get better at getting my scribbled post-it notes in tune.
I was so scared my words would run away in the wake of my father's death,
I didn't write a single thing after completing his eulogy,
After casting that deep-sea fishing line into the dark side of my pale moon.
Took me a thousand years to do that low-gravity bunny hop
Down the crater of my grief and clamber
Somewhere back near where my sentences stopped.
See, I'm afraid I talk too much,
And before waiting for any replies,
I'm already starting to apologise for the space
My conscious stream takes up -
Makes steam rise from some deep shameful place,
Like you could sip my anxiety from your morning coffee cup.
I never mastered the art of succinct communication,
I always feel like my words are suffocated and strangulated.
My fear is a choke-hold.
When I say I'm afraid, I mean I'm jumping at my own shadows,
Startled by my own tornadoes -
Yes, I am afraid of the dark, but I'm also afraid of *my* dark -
The deep uncharted out-of-my-depth -
Like swimming out just far enough that suddenly my feet get cold,
And remembering that last week I sold my last life raft
Because I was certain I could float
On my own oil slick surface and not burn.
Yes, I *am* afraid of my sky falling,
But more afraid of feeling the entire Universe

[...]

48

Turn on a pin head inside me,
Knowing I am vastly unqualified to feel the vastness of that orbit.
Yes, I'm afraid to sit in silence because
What if my silence doesn't want me?
I am so afraid of falling that I will stand in the way of my own gravity,
Clutching for dear life at every poem I write
Like they might teach me something,
But I learnt the Greek word for poem means "made thing"
So I'm learning to be good with my hands,
I'm trying to be better at forming castles in my own wet sand,
I'm trying to stand on all my rickety tables and forget it'll hurt if I fall.
Yes, I am afraid of it all,
But somewhere in my deep, cold-feet, moon-crater dark,
My paper-doll heart sighs,
And while all the panic and all its echoes scream "*run*",
Instead, like the sun,
I'm trying to stay,
And rise.

Stars

My heart is a comet,
A chaos of battered ice trailing bright tails across bruised skies,
All contradiction and complication and old pain
Hurtling a billion miles an hour around the sun,
Screaming "Wait! This heart is too soft a thing
To be thrust so fast into such a violent spin!"
Comets spell omens of disaster from the misplaced letters of 'bad star',
I guess that makes sense - humans are terrible messengers,
We never remember the right parts,
And every pass close to the sun melts another frozen moment,
But I can't figure out what to hold on to and what things to let fly.
Newton said humans have never figured out
How to get somewhere without leaving something behind -
The defined features of a face, a laugh,
The quiet murmur of a half-song sung low,
The tastes and glow of a hundred hot simmering summers,
But what am I if not striving to move forward?
So these memories are flung towards pulsars shimmering
Faster than hummingbirds - -
And they slide unheard into the bell jar of a black hole.
If my heart is a comet, then you are a star.
I look up to give myself a sense of being small,
To find something otherworldly in the wilderness,
To feel the vast eye of all the Universe peering down at me,
But so many of those souls went dark billions of years
Before their light reached me,
This light the last proof they were once alive.
I sleep beneath a graveyard,
I'm staring at a sky full of ghosts,
Making wishes on the bones of the dead,
But you...you are still gone,
And I am still here, getting smaller every year.

Hurricanes & Garden Gates

I have become a conflict zone,
And when I say "my heart is torn apart" I do not mean
I have forgotten how to love,
I mean:
My soul is a no-fly zone and I, a refugee,
Am seeking my truth, my flag, my silent secret song.
My conviction plays an unending game of here and gone,
Of hide and seek,
Of yeses and noes,
To keep me on my toes and keep my dreams in check.
See, this cone around my neck
Shows you I've been licking at self-inflicted wounds,
And soon my own division bell will be the only skin left to peal.
My indecision and anxiety has kept me semi-transparent and barely real,
A pale sighing ghost flailing tragically,
A badly placed metaphor implying
My courage has long been locked in a room behind a door
In a house I'm not sure I ever lived in before.
You see,
My whole life I've been a hurricane without a name,
Constantly downgrading myself to a tropical storm,
Always sure everyone must know I lack form or function,
And yet I am still splitting into all my constituent parts,
Gilding my heart behind an ornate gothic gate.
Yes, the gate is beautiful,
(I'm an artist after all)
But so is the wild, untamed garden beyond the wall,
So pardon me for trespassing on my own unfurled, unkempt lawn.
It dawned on me quite suddenly -
I need to get out of my own way,
Stop laying waste to my sense of self,

[...]

Stop hoarding cans on this shelf and waiting for my own apocalypse,
Stop trying to trip myself up and push myself out,
Stop lying in wait for my own self-doubt,
Stop sneaking sips from the glasses labelled "half-full"
To make them say "drought",
Stop letting the second guessing out of the bag,
Stop snagging that bag on every door frame I try to pass through,
Because I'm done with that game.
I'm starting to sing a song that sounds a lot like it might be
My own true silent name,
Loud,
So it echoes across the floors and chambers of all my hearts.
I'm running barefoot, unlocking all those doors too.
Last night I heard those same hurricane songs
Burn their words in winds and flame,
Each flame wrote their secrets on the stone lodged in my throat,
Each secret a million Gods trapped behind that stone,
Each secret a million suns bursting supernovae beneath my skin,
As they begin the slow spiral of a million Universes
Swirling in my capillaries.
Sing out, wild fire, and call my feet to dance.
Glance at the tiny sparks of light skittering away from me,
This flame of my own god-damn self-raising, self-praising song
Finally fills me right up like a warm drink on the longest coldest night -
Burns,
The way coming in from the perfect snow storm hurts -
A glow,
That shows my soul how to feel whole,
Makes it something I want to belong to,
And when I say "my heart is home", I mean
It makes my matchstick fingertips ache
Because they finally found something worth hanging onto.

A Life Less Travelled

You've got these caged Faraday hands,
You cup lightning and sip it without
Implicitly implying
The sky was lying when it
Said its flash-bombs would burn
Life into dying limbs.
You always have to go that extra mile
To prove a point on a broken arrow.
You yearn for wild and free,
Wound up in the bureaucracy of
Commutes and white shirts.
This shit hurts to walk away from,
It's like scraping off layers of sediment long
Compressed into limestone,
But staying in the cage won't
Quiet the rush of blood in your veins that
Shouts "Come away!",
This equilibrium is coming undone,
A life of regret is more stifling than wild fire smoke.
Don't choke on the wanting.

One Of Us

The roots of my family are not welcome
On the shores of this green and pleasant land.
A fourth generation immigrant, I'm not sure where I stand.
My great grandmother arrived from Malta,
Hoping to alter the course of her destiny.
She split the sea in two only to have doors slammed by
You, ham fisted, talk of immigrants the way you spit the taste of fear.
Don't tell me it shouldn't bother me 'cause I'm from here.
My mother blood bristles at your panic,
It tastes like copper pennies and blood.
The accent dripping from my tongue,
The colour of this skin,
Sufficient to pass your trial-by-sight and fit in,
But give me two weeks in the sun and my skin blossoms mahogany.
Would you still speak to me then?
Where is your line in the sand?
On which side of it do I stand?
"We're not like them, are we?" you tell me.
Your disgust at the brown earth skin seared into my genetic tree,
Your distrust coats my shaking palms
While you calmly and happily sit next to me and curse the others.
Don't tell me there is no room here for them,
When them is me.

Old Song, New Tiki Torches

The ungodly horror of being alive in this time
So full of hate,
This time where we are forced to wait
To see
What fresh wound
Smears and finger paints
And stains our sheets,
What old wound festers on our streets
Unchecked,
Gouged open,
Divided,
Collided.
Strange fruit a thing
I thought long rotted
Still swings.
The star of David still sings the smoke songs of the camps.
The iron still clamps down.
Still, we drown.

All Along The (Ivory) Watchtower

If you have never had your words ripped from your mouth
Before you've even had a chance to speak,
Your thoughts ripped from your lungs
Before you had a chance to breathe -
If you have never stumbled over the answer
To the question mark in the branch of your ancestry,
Nor shuddered at the touch of cold metal at your wrist
Insisting it creep along the crawling of your skin
Simply for being...just *being* and having only just begun,
Nor seen your brothers' abrupt full stop
At the end of a smoking gun -
If you have never had your body smeared
Upon a butchers' block,
Been forced to shut your screams inside a box,
Nor had your worth weighed up and found wanting
Just for honouring the skin inside which you have dared make a home,
Had your aptitude ignored by ineptitude,
Your long list of achievements met with
Raised eyebrow and air of "not bad for a
[delete as appropriate, and so many are nothing
if not empty spaces that remain]" -
If you have never, when choosing a destination,
Had to consider the safety in holding your lover's hand in public,
Or had to hide the exquisite perfect flower of your identity
In the floodlit interrogation of a public bathroom,
If you have never had a job application ignored
Or your existence written off
Just by the rhythm flowing through your name,
Or by the children that you might maybe have one day,
Or the children you'll never have any day,
Or because your body just doesn't do what other people's bodies do -

[...]

If you've never felt the weight of being demanded to prove
Yourself every step of your god-damn way,
Well then, welcome to the top.
I hope you appreciate the view.
I hope you appreciate the tools handed you
That many were not.
I hope you know you're here but for the grace of all the rest.
It really is the best view in town,
You couldn't want for more.
Just remember to check that exquisite privilege at the door.

Army Of Me

The day I discovered Spanx underwear
I swear I actually thanked the gods of elastane
And did a little dance of joy.
Boy, no one could say they were sexy,
Imagine them messaging me:
Hey baby, what are you wearing?
Oh just my comfort-shaping figure-hugging,
Fat-busting, up-round-my-armpits
High-waisted, body-forming, big lady pants
With reinforced girdle...
No.
But that was a hurdle I was willing to take,
A sacrifice I'd been told to make,
To take this space I occupied and... shrink it,
To think it was the worst thing I could be,
To just be *all* of me.
Re-learnt my identity:
"Hello, my name is Fat",
No one will want you like...*that*.
No one will notice the gentleness of your eyes
When your thighs rub together.
You might be funny, kind, creative and clever,
But that doesn't matter.
10 tips for styles that flatter,
10 tips to get thin quick,
To have clear skin,
To make him want you,
Because what are you if he doesn't want you?
Fashion-mag guilt instilled,
Certain the size of my thighs the only thing they'd see,
Trying to quiet this running commentary,

[...]

Every failed fad diet just fuelling this knowledge that
I could never *be* enough
And yet always *too much*.
Have you any idea how tiring that can be?
Always stuck between a rock and a dichotomy?
I'm finally seeing
All that I am is all I can be,
And all I should be,
And maybe that could be *enough*.
A novel idea,
But fear is a tough drug to give up.
It took a whole heap of falling apart to start to begin
To stop thinking this space I take up is a sin.
My bones are steel struts that run deep
To keep me upright in the dark of the night
Under the weight of hate I've collected
Like soft worn over-read pages of poetry
And misplaced guilt.
I have built battalions from words carved
Into this flesh,
Every fresh assault on this body
Reminding me
My breasts do not need scaffolding.
Tell me
My hips swerve like jazz,
I'll tell you I've got curves you can jack-knife on.
I am done being your puppet, your pawn,
I rise with my own dawn, see?
Finally,
Watch me dance unapologetically,
Because my big wide mind cannot handle
The narrow column inches of magazine negativity.
In case you misunderstand,
Here I stand, filling my space,
An army of me.

Strong Women

It is Christmas Day / Eleven days after my Father has died / Three days after my twenty-ninth birthday / Three hours after I have come as close as I hope I ever will to a complete hysterical meltdown that will leave me with mild PTSD / Three hours after I felt the beast of Grief crawling up my throat in a howl I somehow managed to trap / Three hours after leaving my also-very-sick Grandmother (and mother of my just-dead-dad) / I have spent the morning with her - she does not know what day it is / I cooked her food that smelt of hospitals and death / She calls my Mother's house as we step through the door to ask me to come fix her TV / I feel the tremor of the shriek start somewhere near my knees and rip its way up my spine / I threaten to rip the phone lines from the wall / I cannot bear to be in that house a single moment more / Waiting for my Grandmother to call again and again to ask me where my Father is / It is the worst day of my entire life / So we escape and / Three hours later, I am standing in the kitchen of my Mother's sister's house helping with the dishes / My Aunt, tall and strong and pink-haired and tattooed at 63 / Asks me how I'm doing / I shrug / "We aren't the type of women to weep and wail, are we?" She says / And I think - I might be / If I had the time / If I could catch my breath / If the scent of death didn't leak out of every pore / I might / I might weep and wail and fall to my knees and ugly cry / With snot dripping in my hair / If I could just get a hold of my senses for one minute / I wouldn't care / About the marble pedestal the women in this family have long clung to / In every howling gale / I might shave my head and paint my face with ash / Leave my mouth a gash / A slack little "o" of horror / I might run away to an ashram / Or a monastery / Or a cave in the truth of my black mountains / I might shut myself away in a temple to my bottomless despair / And count prayer beads until the wounds began to heal / In some cultures, they mourn for thirteen days straight without a break / They cover mirrors / They do not shave / They burn pyres and candles and incense and they weep / Loudly / They keen / They bleed their sorrow through

[…]

gritted teeth / I think - after so many years of hurting / After I have dragged myself through razor wire / Carried my fallen on flayed shoulders / After the depression and the fear and the cancer and the cancer and *the cancer* / (then the stroke) / And the death / And the funeral arrangements and the probate and / My arthritic Mother being a lost child in a snow drift / And now my sparrow-boned Grandmother haunting the phones every hour of this nuclear winter / It might be nice to catch my breath / For it to not be a failure / To let myself weep and wail / But I don't / So when you tell me I am strong / When you tell me you don't know how I have held it together / How you couldn't do what I have done / I will tell you that this is how a shrapnel wound becomes an amputation / It will take me nearly three years to tell you I wish I hadn't held onto it all so tightly / The art of freefall is a direction, after all.

Weighted

There is no escaping the
Sharp edge of a soft lie.
Open me with a butter knife.
Slip under my edge and slide.
"I'm OK" and "I'm fine" are
Feather-light lies.
Keep me tied around your wrist
So tight,
Anchor me by the kite tails of my fear.
Don't you ever let go,
Do you hear?
I wear my heart on my sleeve.
Please don't ask me to staunch the flow
Right when I'm showing you where I bleed.
Ruby ribbons run from my heart
To my hand
To my page,
Weaving me into the fabric of this place,
Begging me to stay.
I have never found a sunset I haven't wanted to crawl inside,
Even after my worst days.
Sometimes living in the aftermath of my own history
Has been the highest price to pay,
But I'll keep bankrupting myself
To see all that good light
At the end of each day.

Dark Necessities

The deep thrum of bass and drum
Pulses through feet.
Always a feel of the underground, like
We, the discarded lost and found,
Can only repair the bullet holes in our souls
With secret rebellious hidden sound.
A field that ripples and breathes as one,
With sweat and all those dishevelled dreams.
The wail of guitars threatens to
Tear you apart at the seams,
But maybe that isn't a bad thing
If your stitches itch and need unpicking,
And all the things you don't know how to feel
Are pulled up through you with the
Howling anguish of a voice.
It is not a choice to splinter and shatter.
The music that really matters
Teaches you dark backroom truths,
Proof you were forged in fire,
Something in the wiring
Bypasses the brain and speaks to the scar tissue
Of wounds long past their mend-by dates,
A hand thrown out to catch you.
The music moves the immoveable,
And the ringing of that shift
Will still echo in your ears years later
If you listen hard enough.

People Will Sing

One of my best mates boxes.
He gets up early on Sundays and makes his way to the gym
To spar with a kid five times the size and half the age of him.
He says they taught him to keep his eyes open when he gets hit,
And that shit just hit me in the gut like -
We can stare down a fist but we close our eyes when we kiss?
Like, we can sit at the table with own our violence but
We can't bear to be in the same room as our own gentleness.
It's these kind of dichotomies that keep me awake at night, you know?
Like how we really only come together for
Weddings or funerals or sporting events,
And the rest of the time we're all just sort of
Circumventing our hearts in little ships built of Lego parts -
Sharp at the edges but still threatening to break apart.
Gets me thinking about how we're all of us
Breaking apart in to jagged edged pieces,
Like we can swear - all life is sacred,
And in the same breath refuse a hand to those clawing at life
With brittle bones where their hope used to be.
Like how we can march in solidarity,
Wearing our weary worn-down badges of me too, *me too*,
Swearing that this year is the year of the feminist choices -
Yet still chew off our tongues to spite our voices.
How we can find grace in a blade of grass,
Say we can hear God's voice in the vastness of an autumn sky,
Yet still spit blood and rain hate down in
His, or Hers, or Their name,
Like the Divine would never think to ask us why
The beauty and grace and love in the setting sun is not enough.
How can little girls crying ash in mortared schools not be enough?
The faceless mob, the accusing gaping maw,

[...]

64

The groping sweaty paw, the hooligan, the yob,
The police officer "just doing their job",
That tiny spark that throws the protest over the edge into riot,
The awful quiet that falls in the bathroom stalls
When someone who doesn't fit a mould is told they don't belong,
Like we can wash our hands in the same room as a bigot,
But we cannot bear to stand, or kneel, in love and solidarity for equality
For fear of losing our seat.
How is it that love is so often on the back beat?
I'm tired, you know? I'm way past the heat of anger, you know?
I'm bruised from this hard cold calculating world
Slapping me one too many times on the arse and calling me a "good girl".
I'm trying to remember Gandhi's words
About how truth and love have always won,
Trying to remember Rumi said
The cracks are how the light gets in,
I'm trying to remember that there *is* light to let in.
It's tough, you know, like I don't have an answer for you.
This world is hard and people are cruel and
People will hate and take and want and break...
But people will sing,
And there is music,
And people will give and people will dance.
Another friend once said there's a dance for everything,
And that's the sort of light I want my cracks to let in.
I want dance parties in my kitchen when my heart is breaking.
I want guitars and camp fires and shitty renditions of Redemption Song,
So I know people will always be singing redemption,
And people will always be striving
To put one foot in front of the other and climb,
Pulling each other up by the boot straps.
People will clap the rhythm of unity and people
Will cry thunder with their eyes wide open like they can
Finally bear to stand in the presence of their own fragility,

[...]

People will rise and bloom into perfect
Broken-open rooms full of sunlight.
We cold, cruel creatures,
We compassionate, resilient creatures.
There is so much hypocrisy
Blanket-stitched into humanity -
My thumbs have grown calluses
From all the sewing and unpicking.
We bruised and salt-stung things,
We fragile things.
Crack open with me and let
All that broken light
In.

War Ship

My hands tie hope in a language I am still learning to speak,
Weaving lifelines along the shoreline of
My anxieties,
But I swallowed the seeds of panic and
Now an oak tree grows in my belly
To help me stay rooted enough to
Withstand all this knowing.
The battle is in the growing
And I am not yet done.
It is hard work convincing my voice
To carry a tune instead of an apology,
But I sing better in the evenings,
When my throat is crusted with all the
Dust of all the things
I refused to say.
You said white girls can't sing the blues,
And that's probably true,
But this bruised heart will still fill the sails
Of honey-soaked war ships set loose.
I am still strong and my voice,
It is still mine to give as I chose.
Do not think that, because you have dared to dip
A toe in my shallowest stream,
You have navigated this vast ocean of me.
My sea storms will lay waste to you,
Shipwrecked but for the
Taste of salt on your wind-burnt lips.
I have beaten my hands bloody
Shattering mountains that rise in my way,
Don't you dare say I don't know how to overcome,
My whole life has been a becoming.

3: Homeward

"There are a thousand ways to go home again."
Rumi

"It's always in the last place you look."
My Mum

Buckle

Darling, there is no great shame in being soft.
Bend with the breeze.
Kindness is not weakness,
Let it bring you to your knees.

This Is The Sea

He sleeps in early October light,
Curled around me like a question mark.
Even though he knows I'm not the answer,
Still, he's not afraid to ask.
Even though he knows I'm not a problem to be solved,
Still, he writes his workings in the margins of my elbows,
My knees,
My chewed down nails,
My sharp and shadowed parts,
And soft folds of an origami heart on my paper sleeve.
He knows he doesn't know why
This early morning silence sputters apologies,
Why sometimes grief stut-stut-stutters in fits and starts,
Why the shoreline of my mind is dotted with rotting warships
Built from the pieces of burnt-out and broken parts.
He calmly collects it all with the wave-smoothed glass
And keeps it safe,
Makes tiny holes to let me breathe.
He sees me,
More naked than I have ever been,
An ear pressed to the beating in my chest and listening for the sea,
And I know I shouldn't need him, or anyone, to set me free,
But maybe it's OK for him to have given me the key.
Maybe I don't need him to save me,
But maybe it's OK to trim our mainsail on this forever of waves,
Sitting beneath this forever of October sky,
While we pry the lid off my shivering firefly heart,
Kept safe in his storm-lantern jar,
Taste the lightning in the air when he tells me
Love, *love*, look – just *look* at all that sea.

From The Ashes

It's not that you've forgotten how to feel,
It's just that scar tissue goes numb after so many years.
If you focus, you can still see the afterglow of all the hands that let go,
Or held on so tight
That you still wake to the choking of them in the night.
There are still things you are too terrified to unpack and know,
So you drag these boxes like Marley's ghost with never a backwards glance.
No wonder you never felt comfortable in your skin,
You never stuck around long enough to unpack
And begin to make it a home.
You never stuck at anything long enough to figure out
How to sit still and grow.
You used to smoke - you said it's what artists do, they burn,
But you yearned for hot ash in your lungs,
Hoped the creeping black tar pit flow
Had begun making its way through your blood like you thought it should.
Then you quit smoking too,
Unsure whether you wanted a post-volcanic fertile rainforest breath,
Or because you couldn't even stick to a long slow death.
The memories remain stained on white cotton sheets -
All the things you should've said
And all the ways you blame yourself instead.
Breathe -
It is not too late to make up a bed and remove the "room to let" sign.
It is so heavy a thing to be this full of fractured life,
But it's time to set that down.
On the days when you forget to breathe,
I know everything feels like now,
But "now" is just temporary fragments that form a whole,
And you are more than the sum of your splintered heart
Spread out in the shattered nows you left behind.
So many bruised, hurt, ruined things here.

[…]

You are only your past in as much as
You're all the photos you ever take that never make it to a profile page.
Your shameful avoidance of your own shielded gaze,
The refusal to see gold in the split skin of your battlefield,
Is not your everything.
You are the song the morning sings every day
It gets a chance to greet the sunrise,
Saying "thank God it's still here to climb into;
Thank god you never got the word goodbye to stick."
You go ahead and quit all the things that don't fit right.
I know…
I know this world is loud and has held blades
Pressed against your holy gates.
I know you think this life too cold-bright-flashing-fluorescent in
A never-ending corridor of doubt.
I know.
I've been there, too.
I have mourned the loss of myself under so many blood moons.
But here -
Press your palm to your chest.
Feel it pressing back.
That's you.
That's alive.
That's lifeforce pulsing ruby,
Pulsing "true",
Pulsing "here",
Pulsing "dance crazy around the kitchen with me
If it helps the fear and sadness shiver into something new,
Something on the way to free".
You go ahead and shed all the skins that are ready to peel,
You feel every inch of every now yet to come
And you breathe that rainforest breath.
You breathe fresh clean cool air from some higher place.
You put that box down, you hear me?
You're home now.
You can stay.

Biophilia

Every fight we ever have is the same fight,
How you are too often a fog that lifts
The minute I stop trying to find you,
And I, the ship that takes too long to turn,
Keep crashing into your rocks.
When will we learn
To stop counting moments on broken clocks,
To talk without the white noise
Of waves breaking before they've formed?
When will we make it past these jagged teeth cliffs
Stiff with sea spray?
When will we learn to say what we mean,
And mean it when we say it?
When will our words melt at the centre of it?
Meet me somewhere in the middle, would you?
Meet me somewhere warm,
And quietly alive,
Instead of this shifting sand dune shoreline,
One day yours, the next day mine.
Build a cabin in the woods, would you?
Not "yours", or "mine",
But ours, once again, and fill it with time.
A moment stretched on and on
To remember our love is birdsong.
Our love is soft rain through branches grown towards each other.
Our love is towards each other,
Not constantly creaking from one storm to the next,
Not constantly battening down the hatches,
Latching on the safety lines,
Not constantly taking turns to be the leaking life raft.
Is it your turn or mine?
Let's be a forest filled with hushed potential,

[…]

Torrential rain eased by these broad leaves,
Your thumbs
Quietening the rushing of my blood,
My skin
Slicked with mud and moss and the smell of green sprung again.
Send some of that soft love toward me,
The way trees communicate without sound,
Whisper secrets fired along shared networks underground.
I'll send some of that soft love back,
So while I'm sat over here sprouting my self-involved shoots,
And you're over there spreading your branches of
Whatever you're growing into,
We're somehow still doing this thing below the surface,
Somehow still navigating through the darkness,
Where you reaching for my hand across the sometimes-desert of our bed
Is us pooling our resources instead.
You can share my air,
You can drink from my roots,
We can be this shared complex organism
Spanning an entire forest floor.
Take anything you need.
Take everything.
It's yours,
Until you can clear your skies,
And meet me in the middle of the wood.
Meet me somewhere warm,
And quietly alive.

To Be Alone With You

Sunday morning silver light
Through curtain cracks
And traffic hum on already-hot tarmac.
The hiss and grind of buses fussing at the traffic lights.
This morning moment of cat and man and me
All pressed together in semi-sleep and half-dreams.
He murmurs, the cat yawns and I
Drink in this peace to quench the restlessness
Swilling in the rusty oil drum of my body.
I am still rolling the feel of this around my fingertips,
Still trying to find the right fit of my skin,
After so many mornings not knowing how to begin
To live inside myself.
So many mornings my panic has been an ocean-deep
Inky cold thing
Dragging on my tailbone,
But in this Sunday honeysuckle sweetness,
I count the miles back in
Eyelash inches.

The Queen Of All Everything

When I grow up I'm going to be an astronaut,
Or a scientist or a hobbit or a sloth.
I'm going to wear a saucepan hat and a robe of blue cloth.
I'm going to grow up to stand with my hands firmly on my hips.
I'm going to be a dusty-kneed crab-apple pixie...
But then somehow along the way I'm going to end up
Sat halfway up the stairs of myself,
Carefully packing moments into snow globes and
Stacking them on shelves,
Carefully alphabetically categorised and marked "fragile".
I'm going to take root every time someone tells me
I'm not enough to be whatever I want to be.
I will weep leaves every time someone tells me I am too much.
One day I'm going to know a tarmac town
Where estate agents go to die,
Where kids get high and sip cheap cider behind the Wimpy,
With their nervous tangled up little laughs with angry little eyes
That knock me back down to size,
Where my voice will crumble its "no" to dust in my throat,
And they'll believe the mocking slithering lies that I begged him for it,
And the cost of those aftershocks will be so high,
And the shame will never quite defrost,
Even after I figure out how to burn the meaning of consent
In ten-foot words across the fence outside his house.
I will still feel the stifling scent of him after twenty years.
It will make the rest of my education one long fearful lesson in anxiety.
I'll be oversized and stretched and wrong and skip so much class
The teachers won't believe I'll pass a single exam,
But I'll ace them all,
Because I'll have been re-teaching myself to breathe all along
And anything after that will be easy.
I'll leave and come back so often

[...]

My Mum will stitch "return to sender" in the back of all my shirts,
But finally, I'm going to wake up one day and find that place
Too short in the legs for me and I'll fly away.
I want to be a dinosaur and roar at the asteroids headed for me.
I want to be the asteroid.
I want to be a hurtling fireball of truth that makes the earth shake.
When I grow up I going to be a strawberry double chocolate
Fudge peanut butter milkshake,
So I can be so delicious and gooey-thick,
And stick to someone's sweet tooth.
I never want my truth to be easy to swallow,
But I'm going to be the reason someone's eyes get wide and fill with joy.
I know I'm going to grow up in the shadow of the things Grief will destroy.
And, listen, I'll be lost and found so many times
That I'll have to get a compass tattooed on my heart
So I can navigate my way back to the start line
Again and again just by the pull in my veins,
But I'm going to grow up and sail into fabulous
Like it's my own personal fucking port in a storm.
I'm going to be a force of nature,
I'm going to pack so much punch into the rattling of your windows,
I'm going to show you all how I can be so broken
And then so open and then
So fixed up with plywood nailed across my battered frames,
Hanging signs saying "business as usual" decorated with fairy lights,
That you'll all be queuing miles to get a seat in my table.
I'm going to grow up to be whole.
I'm going to grow up to be a soul soaking up the damp rot,
And you won't even be able to tell
That there were whole months that screamed "she'll never make it".
I'm going to grow up to fit everything inside this huge bell
That I'm going to keep ringing with all my might,
Like a midnight summer wedding full of fireflies and candlelight.
There will be so much love and so much sky.
I'm going to grow up and I promise
I'm going to be just fine.

And So We Ran Faster

We were tossed together like water and flour,
But rose into phoenixes.
We should get jerseys,
I'll always want you on my team.
I mean I always want you there to play catch with my shattered nerves
And scatter them like poppy seeds,
Because poppies always grow in rubble,
And even poppies bleed
From dark hearts,
Like they know bruises are inevitable after so many false starts.
I'm going to see grass stains on my new boots and think of you,
Because nothing says 'indestructible' like picking ourselves
After every tumble.
You never turned your back, even when I lacked words,
And dreamt in colours swirling from black to blue,
When my whole body was bruised from life
Kicking me too many times in the face.
You showed me the meaning of grace and beauty
Through your green million-mile eyes that never learnt how to lie,
Through your kaleidoscope smile,
Showed me shapes like landscapes that grow inside the mind.
You make me want to climb the mountains of your spine,
Taste sugar-spun synapses just to see how you brain works
And if it all collapses
Like a house of cards under the weight of that guilt you carry,
Like you're married to the ghosts of failures past
And wear your cigarette burn like a caste,
But I read about Karma, and darling, if it's true,
There's four million tonnes of honeycomb and hummingbirds
Being sent in the mail to you.
It is long overdue.
And I hope right now your hope is a kite, gripped tight,

[…]

Like a promise with a hundred thousand miles of string left to unwind,
Like a hundred thousand smiles just waiting to be kind.
Don't ever stop being kind,
Because there are people who will need it,
Like a storm-cloud needs thunder to chase lightning
Just to prove it's fighting back,
And it's a fact that your smile really does light up a room,
Like there's just more room there when you arrive,
Like you make the light strive to shine further,
Like you hold fire in the curve of your palm,
Calmly nurture this glowing ember that makes us remember
We should always be honest.
Honestly.

One More Mile

The colour blue has the shortest wavelengths,
The baby of the rainbow, it's got shorter legs,
Has to run to keep up with the other colours to make up the light,
But blue light gets scattered most by other molecules.
It's why the sky is blue, the ocean too,
And the distant mountains have that dusky hazy blue-ish hue.
Blue light never quite makes it all the way.
That is to say, blue is where the light gets lost.
Blue is the furthest colour, the longest mile, the saddest sky,
Blue sits alone and wonders why,
Tries to write all the "Wish You Were Here's"
But only manages the colour of tears.
Blue sends postcards that only sometimes arrive.
I think that's why we say we're blue when we're lonely, and far away,
When our heart is a bundle of postcards arriving years too late,
Tied with a red ribbon and left at the gate,
Because red is the first colour we see.
Red runs in screaming "Fire! Fire! You're not wanted anymore!"
And blue gets left behind to stack the chairs and lock the door.
But you know what else I learned?
Shades of blue are one of the only colours dogs can see,
Which is why dogs are so full of love.
They bring all that lost light home.
I want to be your only frequency, the only colour you see,
Your lighthouse, your star on a church spire,
Your porch light so you know you're almost home,
So you know you're almost safe.
I will always be setting your place at my table and piling up the food there.
I always make too much,
I never learnt the right amount of love to share so I always overdo it.
I'm like a puppy with too blue-a stare.
Let me bring all the lost love home to you,
Let me be all this light you couldn't see.

Best Of Me

You have been the best of me.
You are the whetstone
Smoothing each ragged breath
Caught in my sandstorm chest.
You leave candles burning
In all your windows
So I can always find you
In my darkness.
You harness the hurricane in me,
Always leave me tea and toast
To warm my brittle bones.
You sail my gunship home.
You are every holy sunrise
In my mourning heart
When I have been sure
The dawn would fail me.
Your hand pressed against the
War between my shoulder blades
Is my safe haven.

Solstice

I was born on the longest darkest night.
I think that's why I've always felt a little far away,
A quiet hibernating heart,
But I'm trying to remember that,
From where I started,
The world can only turn me to the light.

Christmas Lights

These days there are a lot of things that make me happy,
And there are still a lot of things that make me sad.
Christmas lights make me happy *and* sad.
Happy-sad.
It's an oxymoronic verb that means I am
Found-lost
Sleep-awake
Grief-stained and warped around the edges like I've been
Dropped in the bath too many times.
It's early December and I see the first house covered in flashing lights,
I mean *covered*,
Like Santa vomited Christmas from a great height here,
And it hits me, like it always does this time of year.
Freight train flashbacks and pain but...also...for once, not pain.
A soft cinnamon sweetness,
Nostalgia tipped honeycomb gingerbread halcyon days,
Me ripping wrapping paper in my new PJs,
My birthday cards still lined up on the shelf from 3 days previous,
My dad, propped in the doorway,
His hair lopsided and slept in,
Grins nicotine teeth and
He is the love of my 6 year old life.
Almost 32-year old me feels all this and
Takes myself to the nearest DIY Home store I can find,
Just to surround myself with the gaudy baubles,
Trees and twinkle lights
And cry.
When the young kid with the cowlick and the uniform
Comes to awkwardly ask if I'm OK,
I say - I'm just looking,
For better landing strips to guide my heart into land -
It's taken up orbit in my throat, and I can't stand the methanol afterburn.

[...]

87

I'm just looking,
For a way to learn how to feel safe inside my own memories again.
I'm just looking,
'Cause the lights and the fake pine smell
And the dancing Santas and the neon
Are so beautiful it hurts.
He blinks too much and asks in too-rushed words
If I need any help.
Plenty, I think.
I want to tell him he could help me climb inside
This 6-foot Christmas tree made of fibre optic
Colour changing lights if he likes,
The one that smells of hot plastic and
Burnt out nerve endings,
And we could hide there 'til New Year…
Instead, I smile, and tell him I'm all good here.
His relief is palpable as he scuttles away
From the crazy girl crying at the Christmas display.
But there's this lady -
Older, grey and well-worn around the edges like a well-read book.
She's looking at me with this
Mona-Lisa knowing smile.
She gets it.
Happy-sad.
Lost-found,
Bittersweet,
Hidden-known,
And all the while
These Christmas lights guide me home.

Innsæi

My body has been tossed through so many storms,
My legs find it hard to stand.
The land pitches and rolls,
So I fold myself in healing waters.
My scars,
These clusters of dark matter
Somehow holding me together,
Beg for release.
I whisper to the foam
That the waves might free me,
Hold seashells like they might
Just contain the echoes of
This healing for a thousand years.
If you press your ear to them you can hear
All my sinews stitching themselves
Back together.
I float under a blown glass bowl of sky,
Drifting on this borderless sea,
Navigating by starlight
And one quivering compass point
Turning my sights ever
Towards the clear horizon.

Daydreams and Cityscapes

This City wraps me in cathedral light
And laces my blood with life.
We sit, the City and me, in quiet reflection
Beneath the trees
Just starting the closing act of their show,
Teaching us their very best lessons on letting go,
And we ponder the passing of the day,
And all the people with their raincloud faces turned away.
Once, long ago, I sat in this City
Before it was a home to me,
Sat and sipped a coffee with it and it told me
One day I'd step off the blind conveyor belt and see
There are secrets hidden in the cobblestones here
If I would only stop and listen.
The City would wait for me at the turning of my season.
Fourteen years later when life finally brought me to my knees,
The City said *"See?"*
When I clawed my way out of the winter fog
And stumbled blindly from job and familiarity and security,
The City caught me.
The City said *"Breathe.*
We pave our streets with gold from here."
Now I carve a path to the left of fear,
To the right of your Tuesday mid-morning reality.
This City set me free.
This City has sung me lullabies on
Countless nights of darkened alleyways
From patchwork-lit doorways and bus windows steamed
And streaked in rain-blurred traffic lights.
Me and the City, we're all right.
We don't need the lies.
We're wise enough to see through the smoke and mirrors.

[...]

Your cheap tricks are not enough to convince me back
Into the glut of morning rush hour and heatwave delays.
I never did fit comfortably into a mould of nine-to-five.
I'm no longer just surviving,
I'm thriving.
The City slips me another sun-dappled street
And I meet it with a smile.

To Heal

Now we are fluent
In the language of flowers,
Nectar dripping from
Petal-filled mouths,
Thick with the ruby juice
Of the first bloom.
Now we are continents,
Our consonants
Tremble mountains,
Our vowels
Calm forest fires,
Our bodies
Roll oceans,
We have flowed
Into our lands.

Upon Returning Home
(After Neil Gaiman's "Instructions")

And so here you are at last,
Your feet blistered and back tight,
Your legs grown strong and lean
From the journey of so many miles.
Finally slide your bag from your shoulders
And place it by your feet.
Find your keys, long discarded in some pocket.
Throw away the collected bus tickets, leaves, dust,
Memories you no longer need to keep.
Open the door to the place you left so many months, years before,
Smell that old familiar scent.
Take one glance back at the final sunset
Sinking behind the mountains
That you tore your hands apart to climb.
Take the time to watch the wilderness
You've been lost in for so long.
You've learnt to navigate by
The constellations of fear,
By tears in all the wrong places.
You've learnt to read the map of lost highways and strangled years,
Through places you will never remember the name of but
You'll always remember the smell -
Damp decay and rot, hospital food and
Sad forgotten seaside chip shops in land-locked despair.
Stop now and take that last look back at where you've been.
Remember everything, remember it all.
Step inside.
Kick aside the pile of junk mail left unopened in the hall.
Set down your bag.
Remember to unpack it.
There will be socks to wash.

[...]

Grit and trinkets will have accumulated in there -
The seashells and mortar shells,
The shoreline clinging to your worn down the heels,
They all deserve a place on your shelves.
The house is smaller than you recall.
Perhaps you are just bigger now.
Perhaps you have just grown into all your corners.
It is quiet, filled with a strange hushed forest light.
You know now the wild came home before you to pop the kettle on,
And it will live forever in your walls.
Spread out your arms and embrace the time and lessons
Seeped into to your creaking floors.
Breathe now.
Sleep now.
Rest.

Yellow Is A Sunshine Colour

I'm filling up my home with yellow.
I'm filling my lungs with burnished well-worn hellos
Instead of the long drawn out shadow-and-dust goodbyes.
I'm drawing down the sun one golden sunset at a time.
I'm buying armfuls of sunflowers.
I'm adorning myself like a goddess in gold and cinnamon,
Instead of my native black and silver secrets.
I'm filling vases with corn and wheat-grass.
I've started singing in the evenings,
Filling creeping shadows with mellow jazz.
I'm lighting anything that'll burn.
I'm turning sunshine on a dime,
Hoping to unwind the doubt that always
Seems to knot itself in sheepshanks
Beneath my kitchen sink.
I'm drinking amber-coloured rum
In some bar somewhere by a river.
I'm laying honey prayers on parched lips.
I'm dripping butter on every inch of this life like
This August lion is my homeboy.
I'm dancing peacock feathers and pyrite
Somewhere beneath my timid birdcage breastbone.
I am filling my home with so much sunshine,
There's a goddamn rainbow on every surface.

Changeling

I released them all and now,
A row of empty jars line
My open window ledge,
All edges smoothed from the soft rain
Of the magic of change.
All those age-old wounds gone to seed.
Poppy season was short this year.
The ground, for once, refused to bleed.

Author's Notes

The poems in this collection are a selection of around 8 years-worth of writing, with much of it undertaken following the death of my father in 2015. I realised that my grief was dragging up a lot of very deep-seated issues that were demanding my attention. This book chronicles my journey and though I don't know that I can say I am now "healed", I do think I'm able to look myself in the eye without flinching as much. I would like to thank my family and friends who supported me and read every poem I thrust at them throughout this process.

Whilst I know it's common practice for a poet to not explain their creations; to embrace the sense that, once a poem is released into the wild, it ceases to mean what the poet meant when they wrote it and becomes a lens through which any reader can interpret their own meanings and truths... I also really like books that include a bit of background and voice of the author separate to the meaty content – a bit of "behind the scenes" if you will. I've hidden these notes on the poems you'll have (hopefully) read in this back-room of the book so you can read, or ignore, as you prefer.

Section 1 : Lost – The poems in the first chunk of the book weren't all written when I was in the midst of bleak depression, but they are all about that feeling, and are what I'm collectively referring to as "the sad ones".

Jam Jar Heart – This little poem, as ridiculous and cliched as it sounds, came to me in a dream. Fully formed like this. Bam. It's about being afraid to start opening up because - what if you can't stop?

Forecast – I wrote this while watching snow fall in March of 2018. The snow was hard like polystyrene pellets and wouldn't even stick together to make snowballs.

Creeping Dose – Another term for sickness resulting from exposure to radiation. In other words, what chemotherapy and radiotherapy do to the body. My then-boyfriend (now husband) had stage 3 bowel cancer at 27. He is now, almost 8 years later, in remission, but with specific genetic markers that mean he will be susceptible to it coming back again if he's not regularly screened. This was the first long-form poem I wrote in what I guess I can call "my style", after discovering Andrea Gibson and their phenomenal "Photograph".

Way Down We Go – Written way back in the midst of my husband's chemotherapy treatment. It was a lonely time for both of us.

Fever Moon – After the winter that dragged almost to Easter, we had a heatwave that scorched the earth. I often found it hard to breathe at night. I wrote this sat up in the early hours, full of panic at memories shoved into too many boxes in my head.

Precipice – Your mind can only hold so many separate hurts before it all just blurs into one lump. I think I reached a sort of saturation point.

The Marvellous Mechanical Wind Up Man – The first thing I wrote after my Dad died, as a Father's Day gift. 11 weeks is not an exaggeration. Pancreatic cancer is called the silent killer for a reason. Two weeks before his death, the cancer caused him to have a stroke that put him in hospital. He didn't come home.

Roommates – They never paid rent and drank all the milk.

Heart Shaped Box – It's an awful thing to feel like a substitute person, shifting chameleon-like to simply serve what others require of you.

The Exact Shade of Red – This was meant to be a Mother's Day gift. It morphed into something less…pretty. It is terrifying to realise that parents are not, despite my fervent belief, ageless immortal beings designed solely to bring me cups of tea and sausage rolls. I still gave this to my Mum on Mother's Day, and she still loved it.

Rusted – Ruminations on how, every time he goes for a check-up, I panic a bit. Check-ups are good. They mean things will get spotted quickly if there is anything to spot…but they make it all very real again.

Unmake This Wild Light – Written after several panic attacks in a row.

Anxiety 101 – This started out as a message to a friend, sent after said low-level panic attack following the realisation that I was responsible for losing the Holy Grail of umbrellas.

Of Socks and Clocks – It will come as no great surprise to anyone who has read all this that I am an introvert of the highest order. It is a very loud world out there.

Ghosts In The Wall – One of my guilty pleasures is watching paranormal shows. I love them. They make me laugh, but there is also that itching sense of "what if". I wrote this about the women in my family – all "strong" in that 'pick yourself up and get on with things' way. I found an exceptional photograph of my great(x4) maternal grandmother and her sisters, dressed in Victorian dresses, looking very stern, and wrote this poem after binge-watching ghost shows when I couldn't sleep. It's about how I have felt like a failure for being so sensitive and overly emotional, for letting my fears and anxieties crumple me, when they would not have had the luxury to fall apart.

The Woman Who – This started life as a word prompt on Instagram. I feel like it is an older, more mature version of Creeping Dose.

Wilderness Survival Guide – Parts of this came from my own social media statuses and journal entries before being woven into a pseudo-instruction manual on how I survived living on this knife edge of anxiety and depression, and to remind myself that it did pass.

Section 2: Map Reading and Route Finding – The poems in this section are what I think of as the "getting my shit together and getting angry" poems.

Falling Leaves – I have always found it hard to let go. This book is part of that process for me.

Unexpected Roses – When we moved into our new home in September 2017, I discovered a sprawling rose bush in the back garden with the most beautiful roses I've ever seen and smelt just bursting out everywhere. I ventured out into a tundra of uncut grass and brambles at the start of a heatwave just after I had left my job, and spent hours hacking away at weeds.

This Is Fear Country – When I first wrote this, it came in at nearly 6 minutes long when read aloud – there was a LOT that I was afraid of. There's something allegorical in the fact that, during editing, at the end of so much soul searching and therapy, I got it down to two and a half minutes.

Stars – David Bowie was a hero of mine. He passed away a few weeks after my dad. My early grieving was to a Bowie soundtrack and the world felt like it was mourning with me. This is, of course, about my dad, but I wanted to write something applicable to anyone who has ever lost someone. Inspired by Space Oddity by David Bowie, and the 2014 TV series Cosmos: A Spacetime Odyssey, presented by Neil De Grasse Tyson (in particular, episode 4 titled "A Sky Full of Ghosts").

Hurricanes and Garden Gates – Written after a morning of catching my bag on almost everything I tried to walk past on my way to work and thinking very clearly to myself – I need to get out of my own way. Not long after this, I handed in my notice.

A Life Less Travelled – The title to this was inspired by the Robert Frost poem "The Road Not Taken". I quit my job as a consulting transport engineer after ten years because I realised I couldn't breathe anymore.

One Of Us – This is a true story. I am one eighth Maltese. Title inspired by the Joan Osborne 1995 song "What If God Was One Of Us" (which was in fact not written or recorded by Alanis Morrisette despite what your brain might be telling you right now).

Old Song, New Tiki Torches – Inspired by the events of August 11th and 12th 2017, where white supremacists held a "unite the right" rally in Charlottesville, Virginia, USA.

All Along The (Ivory) Watchtower – Title inspired by the 1967 Bob Dylan song made famous (or at least made more familiar to more people) by Jimi Hendrix in 1968. There's a part of me that worries this poem is veering into tokenism given that, as a white straight cis-gendered woman in the western world, I benefit from many privileges not offered to others, so perhaps should not speak of that which I have not experienced, and that perhaps I am trying to avail myself of guilt by speaking for others…but…the poem demanded to be written anyway..

Army Of Me – Title inspired by the 1995 Bjork song of the same name, and inspired in part by Dr. Maya Angelou's "Phenomenal Woman". I have never burnt a bra, but I have thrown out a lot of old Spanx.

Strong Women – One of the very last poems written for this book. It's very raw and real.

Weighted – Another poem that started life as a writing prompt response on Instagram.

Dark Necessities – Music has been a saviour to me. I wrote this after a gig in 2018, but it ended up being about seeing the Red Hot Chili Peppers perform at Reading Festival in the summer of 2016. I first saw the Chili's perform in London in 2011 the day before my partner got his cancer diagnosis. 5 years later, when my partner was well again but my dad had died, they were playing the Reading Festival. I needed to go. The festival fell the weekend after moving my Mum across the country to her new flat. It was like a bookend to all the shit of the intervening years. It was a catharsis, a magic spell I was casting to make sure nothing else happened. It was intense, and joyous. I came down with the flu the next day, because for the first time in 5 years, I let myself relax. The title is from the Chili Peppers track from their 2016 album "The Getaway".

People Will Sing – Written after getting disheartened by the political climate and depressing news. A rallying cry for human kindness.

War Ship – Written following comments from random men on the internet.

Section 3: Homeward – all the slightly less sad, more hopeful poems (and yes, even the odd 'happy' poem) are in the last section of the book.

Buckle – Inspired by something a friend told me; that her Mum was worried she was becoming too hard and cold as she grew older and was losing her innocent "soft" outlook on the world.

This Is The Sea – An anniversary gift for my husband, and inspired by the Waterboys song of the same name.

From The Ashes – A piece I wrote specifically as a spoken word piece from myself to myself, and to anyone else that needs to be reminded to unpack their lives and stay.

Biophilia – This piece was inspired by the 2011 Bjork album of the same name, a fascinating 2016 TEDSummit talk given by Suzanne Simard titled "How Trees Talk To Each Other" and concepts presented in Star Trek Discovery about how living organisms share resources through fungal networks underground. Contrary to popular belief, even happily married couples do still argue occasionally.

To Be Alone With You – Just a love poem.

Queen Of All Everything – I really did want to be a dinosaur. The rest of this is also true.

And So We Ran Faster – Written for a friend that needed to move back home when they were going through a tough time.

One More Mile – This piece was inspired by a Brain Pickings article by Maria Popova titled "Why the Sky and the Ocean Are Blue: Rebecca Solnit on the Color of Distance and Desire".

Best of Me – Just another love poem. Shocker.

Solstice – Unsurprisingly written on my birthday, in 2017.

Christmas Lights – One of the last poems to be written for this book, in the December of 2018, though it had been brewing since Christmas the year before when my bus route home to our new house let me see so many houses decorated and lit up. Inspired a little by Coldplay's song "Fix You".

Innsæi - (pronounced in-sigh-ay) is the ancient Icelandic word for intuition, but has multiple meanings. It can mean "the sea within", "to see within" and "to see from the inside out". The word and concept were discovered via the film of the same name, written by Hrund Gunnsteinsdottir and directed by Hrund Gunnsteinsdottir and Kristín Ólafsdóttir.

Daydreams and Cityscapes – On occasion, I do take myself out of my hermit hole and go out to write. I love walking around the City at mid-morning. This was written in coffee shops and on park benches around Bristol. When I was an unhappy 18-year-old at University in Bath, I visited Bristol for a day to meet my Cousin. I sat in one of those same coffee shops and looked over the river at the building which, 4 years later, I'd end up working in. 10 years after that, I'd sit in the same coffee shop looking at the same building I no longer worked in. It's a funny old world.

To Heal – Inspired by the oldest possession I have – a small book titled "The Language of Flowers" that belonged to my great-great Grandmother.

Upon Returning Home – Inspired by the tone of Neil Gaiman's poem "Instructions" – If you've not read it, go find it. I promise you'll survive every fairy tale once you do. I also wrote this as a sort of sequel/ending to Wilderness Survival Guide.

Yellow Is A Sunshine Colour – Written during the immense heatwave of the summer of 2018 when I really felt things starting to click into place for me emotionally, after taking the time away from the world to write and deliberately work on healing myself.

Changeling – Written, I suppose, as a direct response to the very first poem in this book, Jam Har Heart. A Changeling is a mythical fairy child swapped for a human child.

Playlist

(These songs help shape the poems in this book. This playlist is available to stream publicly via Spotify – search "fear country".)

- The Fear – Robin Loxley
- Small Blue Thing – Suzanne Vega
- Video Games – Lana Del Rey
- Chalk Stars – Animal Kingdom
- I Ain't Scared of Lightning – Tom McRae
- Wish You Were Here – Pink Floyd
- Rocket Man – Elton John
- While My Guitar Gently Weeps (Anthology 3 version) – George Harrison
- Sweet Home Alabama – Jewel
- Unmake the Wild Light – 65daysofstatic
- Ghosts in the Walls – Charles Vaughn & The Daily Routine
- Running Up That Hill – Placebo
- Wild Rose – Will Stratton
- Wet Sand – Red Hot Chili Peppers
- Space Oddity (Live Version) – Natalie Merchant
- My Father's Gun – Miranda Lambert
- One Of Us – Joan Osborne
- All Along the Watchtower – Afterhere
- Army of Me – Bjork
- And Here I Stand – Skunk Anansie
- Everything's Gonna Be Fine – Gabe Lopez
- Got A Suitcase, Got Regrets – Tom McRae
- Dark Necessities – Red Hot Chili Peppers
- One More Time – Daft Punk
- Redemption Song – Bob Marley
- This Is The Sea – The Waterboys
- Ashes – Embrace

- Mutual Core – Bjork
- To Be Alone With You – Sufjan Stevens
- We Were Young (feat. Arc En Ciel) – Moog
- The Queen of All Everything – Ott
- Moonage Daydream – David Bowie
- If You Don't Want To Be Alone – Firehorse
- One More Mile – Tom McRae
- Best of Me – Smyang Piano
- Cigarette Daydreams – Cage The Elephant
- Fix You (Instrumental Music Box) – Baby Lullaby Garden
- Gravity – Embrace
- Orange Sky – Alexi Murdoch
- To Heal – Underworld
- Last Sunrise In The Wasteland – At The End of Times, Nothing
- Yellow Light – Of Monsters and Men
- Walking With Happiness – The Best Pessimist
- Feeling Good – Ane Brun
- Encore – Red Hot Chili Peppers
- He Films the Clouds Pt. 2 – Maybeshewill
- Dog Days Are Over – Florence + The Machine
- Tomorrow's Song – Olafur Arnalds
- I Believe – DJ Khaled, Demi Lovato

About the Author

Alice is a poet, over-thinker, worrier, dreamer, story teller, and story collector. She grew up in Medway and now lives in Bristol, in the South-West of the UK, with a husband and a cat. She is an avid tea-drinker. Alice's poetry often rhymes, but not always, and when it does, not always in the way you think it should. Try not to let this upset you too much. Her work is confessional and maximalist. She hopes you won't hold this against her.

This is her first book.